M

for You
(and other beings)

Laurie Fisher Huck

ELEMENT
CHILDREN'S BOOKS

SHAFTESBURY, DORSET · BOSTON, MASSACHUSETTS · MELBOURNE, VICTORIA

First published in the UK in 1998 by
Element Children's Books, Shaftesbury, Dorset SP7 8BP

Published in Australia in 1998 by Element Books Ltd for
Penguin Books Australia Ltd, 487 Maroondah Highway,
Ringwood, Victoria 3134

Published in 1996 by Weatherhill, Inc, of New York and
Tokyo, 568 Broadway, Suite 705, New York, NY10012 as
MEDITATION FOR KIDS. First published by
Red Dory Press 1993.

British Library Cataloguing in Publication data available

ISBN 1 901881 19 9

Cover design by Ness Wood
Printed in Hong Kong through Worldprint

To anyone brave enough to sit still
for more than ~~twenty~~ minutes.
TEN

Meditation
means
different
things
to
different
people.

(Nothing happens)

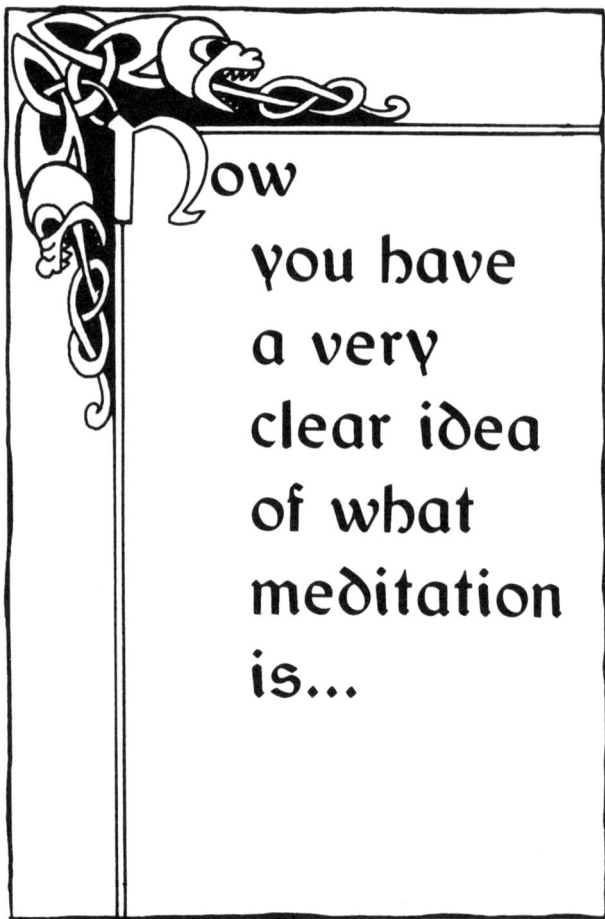

ow
you have
a very
clear idea
of what
meditation
is...

...not!

The
point
is..

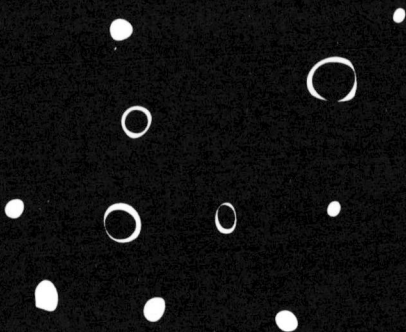

LIFE
IN THE
VAST
LANE

Start—
by taking
a vast
view of
yourself.

You
can
become
wise...

and of
benefit
to this
planet.

If you are:

☐ The popular, super cool type
    or
☐ The cheerful, likeable type
    or
☐ The quiet type
    or
☐ The visitor from planet X type
    or
☐ The bossy pants type
    or
☐ The basketball player type
    or
☐ The save the planet type
    or
☐ The confused and unhappy type
    or
☐ The baseball card dealer type
    or
☐ The love to have fun type
    or

☐ The loner type
    or
☐ The "I wanna run away" type
    or
☐ The gorgeous, too cool to live type
    or
☐ The weirdo type
    or
☐ The neanderthal type
    or
☐ The know all the dinosaurs type
    or
☐ The good at everything type
    or
☐ The hidden genius type
    or
☐ The jog before breakfast type
    or
☐ The artistic type
    or
☐ The I want to make a difference type
    or

☐ The wear only the best gear type
or
☐ The hair obsessed type
or
☐ The can't stop talking type
or
☐ The discipline problem type
or
☐ The "give me a break" type
or
☐ The gotta watch TV type
or
☐ The 50,000 ideas at once type
or
☐ The play the piano *and* violin type
or
☐ The "Archie" comic book type
or
☐ The glued to a computer type
or
☐ The everyone else is weird type
or

☐ The always listening to music type

or

☐ The moody type

or

☐ The grumpy type

or

☐ The star athlete type

or

☐ The world is going to pieces type

or

☐ The do things for others type

or

☐ The travel alot type

or

☐ The have no money type

or

☐ The read this whole list type

or

☐ ALL OF THE ABOVE (depending on day, year, allowance, and latest haircut)

Excellent!

Then you might really enjoy discovering what meditation can be for you.

Sometimes:
wild...

...fun...

Most
of what
happens
in your
life...

starts
in the
ocean
of
your mind.

Thoughts rise like waves and then disappear

Your
mind
is
like
a

horse...

beautiful,
independant,
and
strong.

Being a good rider takes practice

Come Back

There
are
two
things
you
should
know.

You
have a
mind.

It

thinks.

(a lot!)

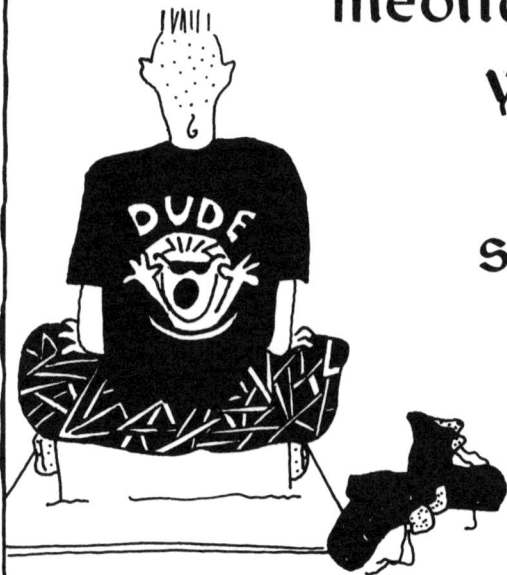

When
you
meditate
you
sit
still

and let your mind relax...

As
your
mind
relaxes...

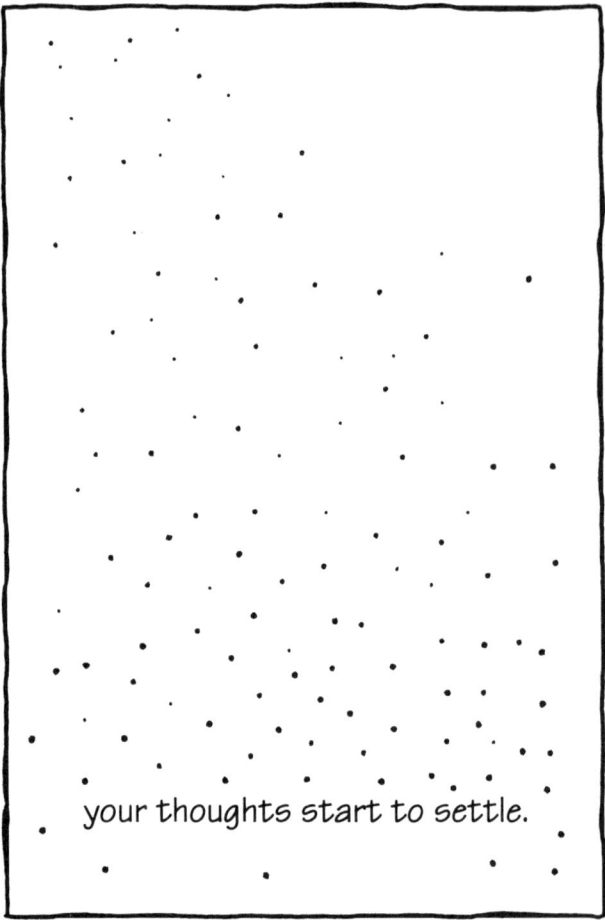

your thoughts start to settle.

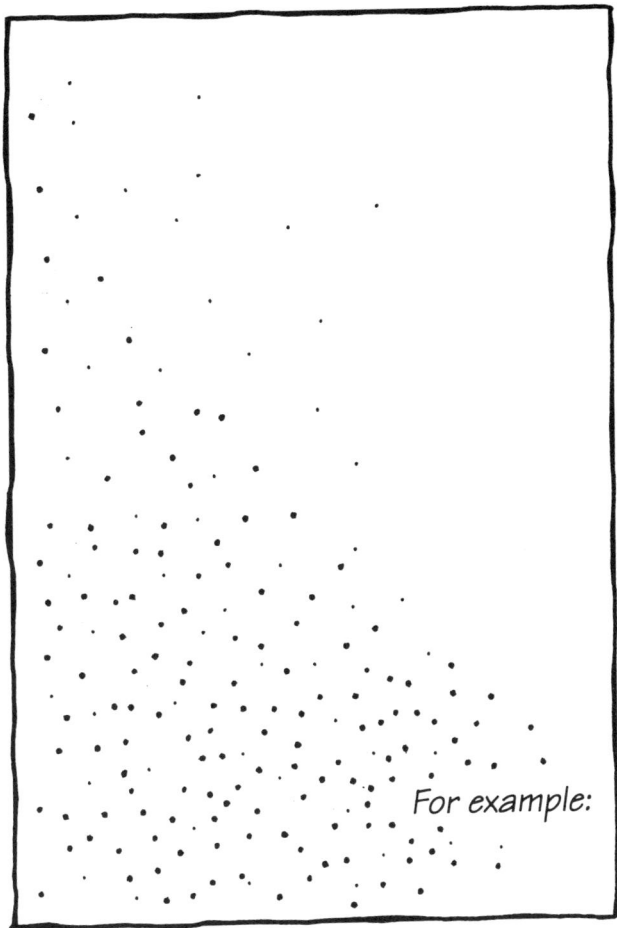

For example:

How
do
you
let
your
mind
relax?

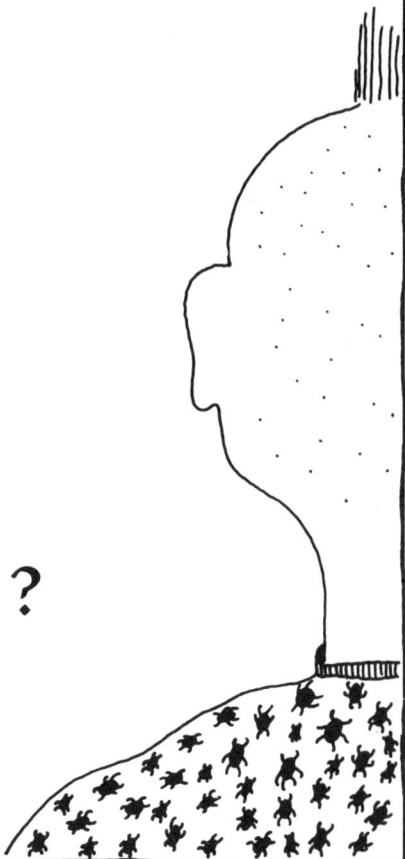

By
not making
a
BIG
DEAL
out of
any
thought.

and come back to
your breath.

sitting
breathing
sitting
...Boy, a peanutbutter
sandwich would sure taste
good. Maybe I'll...
"Thinking"
sitting
breathing
sitting
breathing
sitting
breathing
...Oh yeah. I can't believe
Marlys said that about
me...
"Thinking"
sitting

...I"ll kill her
"Thinking"
breathing
sitting
...With a gun
"Thinking"

...Better yet, a machete!
"Thinking"
           sitting
           breathing
           sitting
...It's quiet in here
"Thinking"
           breathing
           sitting
           breathing
           sitting
...YIKES!! I didn't get my
money from Mrs. Row and...
"Thinking"
           breathing
           sitting

...WHEW!! That must be
what...
           "Thinking"
           breathing
           sitting
           breathing
           sitting
...My butt hurts.
                    ad nauseum...

Boring?

Yes, but...

real.

The funny
thing about
meditation is:
you start
wanting
to
do it.

Maybe
you begin
to notice
that
coming back
feels better
than
not
coming back.

When you are:

happy
confused
angry
sad
excited
thrilled
fuzzy-minded
brilliant
lost
irritated
nervous
spooked
confident
unsure
guilty
delighted
just plain weird

→ *whatever...*

Just
sit.

Come
back
to
where
you
are.

There's
no
place
like
it.

Picture of the author

Before 10 years
of meditation.

After 10 years of
meditation.